THIS IS A WELBECK CHILDREN'S BOOK
Published in 2020 by Welbeck Children's Books Limited
An imprint of the Welbeck Publishing Group
20 Mortimer Street, London W1T 3JW
Text, design and illustration © Welbeck Publishing Limited 2020
ISBN: 978-1-78312-536-4

Writer: Simon Mugford
Designer and Illustrator: Dan Green
Design manager: Emily Clarke
Executive editor: Suhel Ahmed
Production: Nicola Davey

A catalogue record for this book is available from the British Library.

Printed in the UK
10 9 8 7 6 5

Statistics and records correct as of 1st January 2020

FOOTBALL SUPERSTARS

KANE

RULES

SIMON MUGFORD   DAN GREEN

CONTENTS

CHAPTER 1

Amazing Kane

HARRY KANE! HARRY KANE!

Harry Kane is an *INCREDIBLE,*

AWESOME FOOTBALLER.

He is the **ENGLAND CAPTAIN** and one of the best strikers in the **WORLD.**

SO WHAT MAKES **KANE** SO BRILLIANT?

Height
Tall and strong, great at headers.

Power
One of the most powerful shots in the game.

Accuracy
Always gets his shot on target.

Vision
Creates chances for his team-mates.

GOALS!
The **REALLY IMPORTANT** bit.
He **SCORES LOADS OF GOALS!**

Harry is simply **INCREDIBLE** in front of goal.

THE ULTIMATE STRIKER!

9

TO SEE HOW GOOD KANE IS, LET'S HAVE A LOOK AT HIM IN NUMBERS . . .

6 . . . Premier League Player of the Month awards

2 . . . Premier League Golden Boot awards

1 . . . World Cup Golden Boot award

32 . . . goals for England

KANE I.D.

NAME:
Harry Edward Kane

NICKNAME:
The Hurricane

DATE OF BIRTH:
28 July 1993

PLACE OF BIRTH: *Walthamstow, London, England*

HEIGHT: *1.88 m*

POSITION: *Centre-forward*

CLUBS: *Tottenham Hotspur*

NATIONAL TEAM: *England*

LEFT OR RIGHT-FOOTED: *Right*

CHAPTER 2

YOUNG HARRY

Harry Kane was born in **Walthamstow,** in north-east **London,** in **1993**. He lived there with his mum and dad, and his older brother Charlie.

Harry's family **LOVED** football. And they all supported a team that was just a few miles down the road from Walthamstow:

TOTTENHAM HOTSPUR

Charlie →

Harry

Harry and Charlie played football any time they got the chance. Charlie would make **Harry play in goal** and take shots at him.

HARRY WAS A GOOD GOALKEEPER!

I was a goalkeeper for my school team.

Cool. Were you any good?

Not really. The only thing I caught was a cold!

Teddy Sheringham

But Harry wanted to **score goals.** He wanted to be a **striker** and **play for** *TOTTENHAM.*

When **Harry was six,** his family moved a few miles away to **Chingford.** He had a trial for a local team,

RIDGEWAY ROVERS.

At first, Harry played in goal...

David Beckham played for Ridgeway Rovers, too.

. . . **but when the coaches** made him a forward, *HE SCORED A HAT-TRICK!*

Harry was **determined** to be the ***BEST.*** He would **practise and practise** with Charlie and his dad, or play with his **friends at the park.**

They played in the street, too. They had to stop for cars of course, but **Harry loved street football.** It taught him to be *QUICK* and *MOVE* in tight spaces.

That kid's good.

He'll play for England one day.

When he was **eight,** Harry joined the
academy at a top **Premier League Club**
- Tottenham's north London rivals:

ARSENAL!

He **played a whole season** for the Gunners. Harry scored **lots of goals,** but Arsenal said he needed to get *BIGGER AND STRONGER.*

NEVER MIND, SON. YOU'RE TOO GOOD FOR THEM ANYWAY!

Harry's dad
(Spurs fan)

Harry was sad, but he soon **cheered up.** *RIDGEWAY ROVERS* were happy to **have him back!**

Harry kept on playing for Ridgeway Rovers.
He trained REALLY hard.

When he was **11**, Harry spent a few weeks
at Watford. Then finally, **Harry's dream
came true.** He went to play for

TOTTENHAM HOTSPUR!

CHAPTER 3

SPURS AT LAST

In the UNDER-13 team at Tottenham, all the other players were much ***BIGGER*** and ***STRONGER*** than Harry.

But Harry **trained** and **practised** more than anyone else. The coaches saw how hard he worked and kept him on.

At 15, Harry was starting to grow into a much **STRONGER,** better player. He played in under-16 tournaments in **Mexico** and **Switzerland.**

On **28 July 2009**, Harry signed an academy **contract** with Tottenham.

IT WAS HIS
16TH BIRTHDAY
AND THE BEST DAY
OF HIS LIFE!

Harry scored **18 goals** in **22 games** for the under-18s in 2009-10.

He was on **FIRE** as a **STRIKER!**

Did someone say **FIRE?**

WATER

Harry started training with star players like **Gareth Bale, Luka Modrić** and his goalscoring hero, **Jermain Defoe.**

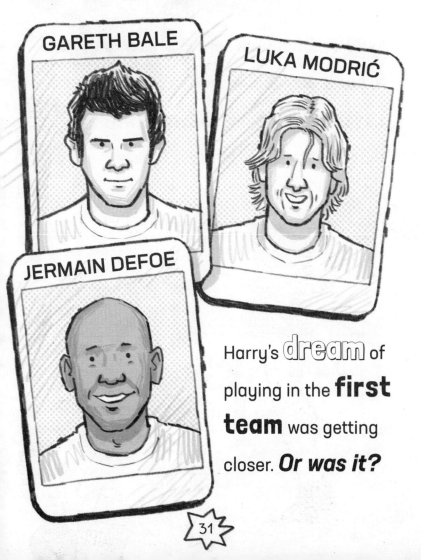

GARETH BALE

LUKA MODRIĆ

JERMAIN DEFOE

Harry's **dream** of playing in the **first team** was getting closer. *Or was it?*

LONDON
LOANS

In 2011, Tottenham sent Harry out **on loan** to two lower-league London clubs –

Leyton Orient and **Millwall.**

Harry worked hard to prove himself.

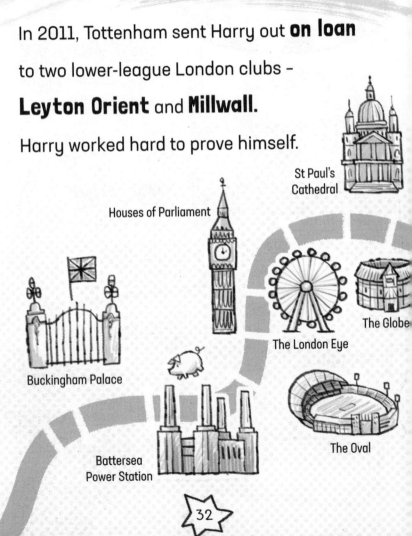

St Paul's Cathedral

Houses of Parliament

The Globe

The London Eye

Buckingham Palace

The Oval

Battersea Power Station

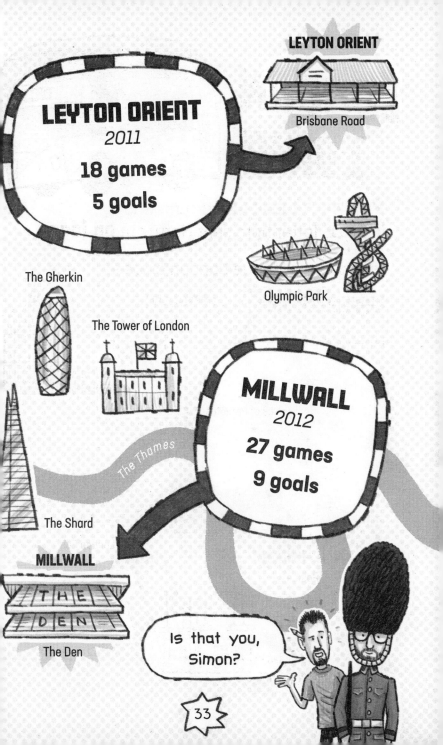

Harry was loaned out twice more, first to **Norwich** and then to **Leicester.** Then, ***FINALLY,*** he made his first **Premier League** start for Spurs, against **Sunderland** on 7 April, 2014.

In the **59th minute, Harry scored!** He couldn't believe it and **celebrated wildly** with his team-mates!

HARRY HAD ARRIVED!

For the **2014-15** season, Tottenham had a new manager, *MAURICIO POCHETTINO.*

Pochettino gave Harry more games. The more he played, the more

GOALS HE SCORED!

THE TOTTENHAM FANS HAD A NEW HERO AND A NEW CHANT:

KANE RULES

HE'S ONE OF OUR OWN,

HE'S ONE OF OUR OWN,

HARRY KANE –

HE'S ONE OF OUR OWN!

Harry ended **2014-15** with an incredible **31 GOALS** in all competitions and was named as the: **PFA YOUNG PLAYER OF THE YEAR.**

IT'S AN INCREDIBLE, **INCREDIBLE** FEELING. THIS SEASON HAS BEEN **UNREAL.**

CHAPTER 4

LONDON LEGENDS

39

Harry followed in the footsteps of football legend, *DAVID BECKHAM.*

BeCkHAM . . .

. . . started out at Ridgeway Rovers, *JUST LIKE HARRY.*

COOL HAIR!

. . . went to Chingford Foundation School, *JUST LIKE HARRY.*

41

In 2005, **David Beckham** started his **Football Academy.** **11-year-old Harry** was one of the schoolchildren invited to the launch.

HE WAS MASSIVELY EXCITED TO MEET HIS HERO!

HARRY'S CLASSMATE KATE WAS THERE, TOO.

Harry and Kate got married in *2019.*

Aw, that's so sweet!

43

LOCAL HEROES

These players were **all born** and grew up around **CHINGFORD.**

David Beckham

Manchester United, Real Madrid and England icon

Teddy Sheringham

Tottenham and Manchester United legend

CHAPTER 5

PREMIER CLASS

PREMIER LEAGUE 2014-15

KEY MOMENTS FROM HARRY'S BREAKTHROUGH SEASON.

1 JANUARY 2015

Tottenham 5-3 Chelsea

Harry won a penalty and scored two goals to help Spurs beat their London rivals in this thriller.

BOP!

7 FEBRUARY 2015

Tottenham 2-1 Arsenal

Arsenal were ahead after 11 minutes, but Harry's two goals gave Spurs a memorable derby win.

21 MARCH 2015

Tottenham 4-3 Leicester City

Harry's 64th-minute penalty completed his first Premier League hat-trick in this goalfest against Leicester City.

PREMIER LEAGUE 2015-16

HIGHLIGHTS OF A SPECIAL SEASON FOR HARRY.

26 SEPTEMBER 2015

Tottenham 5-1 Manchester City

Harry's 61st-minute strike against Man City kick-started his goalscoring for the season.

50

Dele Alli

19 DECEMBER 2015

Southhampton 0-2 Tottenham

This was **Harry's 100th appearance** for Spurs and the start of his partnership with Dele Alli.

2 APRIL 2016

Liverpool 1-1 Tottenham

Harry's goal made him Tottenham's top scorer in a single Premier League season.

GREATEST GOAL #1

3 MARCH 2016

Tottenham 2-2 Arsenal

Dele Alli flicked the ball on to Harry who then curled in a fantastic shot from an impossible angle.

ONE OF HIS BEST EVER GOALS.

Harry was wearing a face mask because of a nose injury, but he took it off as he ran to *CELEBRATE* in front of the fans.

FIRST GOLDEN BOOT

Harry ended **2015-16** as the **PREMIER LEAGUE'S TOP SCORER,** winning his first Golden Boot.

This golden boot is a bit heavy!

54

PREMIER LEAGUE TOP SCORERS 2015-16

HARRY KANE
TOTTENHAM HOTSPUR
25 GOALS

SERGIO AGÜERO
MANCHESTER CITY
24 GOALS

JAMIE VARDY
LEICESTER CITY
24 GOALS

Harry was the **first Spurs player** to win the Golden Boot since his hero **Teddy Sheringham,** in 1992-1993.

He was also the first *English* player to win since Sunderland's *Kevin Phillips* in *1999-2000!*

CHAPTER 6

HARRY'S
HEROES

One day, when Harry was 11, he was playing a five-a-side game with his friends. A man pulled up in a cool car and said hello – it was the **Tottenham** striker **JERMAIN DEFOE** – one of **HARRY'S BIGGEST HEROES!**

Jermain even joined in their game!

Harry and his friends could not believe it.

Harry reminded Jermain about this game when he joined Spurs!

59

When Harry was little, **Jürgen Klinsmann** was the top striker for Spurs.

In **2014**, Harry celebrated an important late goal against **Aston Villa** with Klinsmann's famous celebration –

THE KLINSMANN DIVE.

Harry is a **BIG FAN** of *AMERICAN FOOTBALL* and says that **NFL** star **Tom Brady** has inspired him.

Tom Brady

Brady had to **work hard** to prove how good he was and get to the top of his game –

JUST LIKE HARRY.

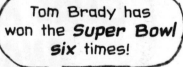

Harry has even said he'd like to play as a **kicker** in the **NFL!**

Tom Brady has won the **Super Bowl six** times!

CHAPTER 7

GOLDEN GREAT

PREMIER LEAGUE 2016-17

HIGHLIGHTS OF ANOTHER FANTASTIC SEASON.

01 JANUARY 2017

Watford 1-4 Tottenham

Harry marked his **100th Premier League** appearance with **two** goals against Watford.

26 FEBRUARY 2017

**Tottenham 4
Stoke City 0**

*Harry was in incredible form, scoring his **third** hat-trick in **nine** games.*

15 APRIL 2017

Tottenham 4-0 Bournemouth

*Returning from injury, Harry scored his **20th Premier League goal** of the season.*

PREMIER LEAGUE 2016-17

In **May 2017,** with two games left to play, Harry had scored **22 league goals.** Then . . .

he scored an incredible **FOUR** goals as Spurs beat Leicester City **6-1** . . .

. . . and then scored a **hat-trick** as **Hull City** were thrashed **7-1!**

Harry's **SEVEN** goals in **TWO** games sent him to the **top of the scoring table:**

HARRY KANE
TOTTENHAM HOTSPUR
29 GOALS

ROMELU LUKAKU
EVERTON
25 GOALS

ALEXIS SÁNCHEZ
ARSENAL
24 GOALS

And he won his second Golden Boot!

AMAZING
ACHIEVEMENT

HARRY was the **top Premier League scorer** after only **30** appearances.

He missed eight games through injury.

He scored **THREE** league **hat-tricks**.

Tottenham finished **SECOND** in the league. It was their **best** position for **54 years.**

Across all competitions, Harry scored **35 goals.**

Harry was the **FIRST PLAYER** to win **TWO GOLDEN BOOTS** in a row since Robin van Persie in **2013**.

CHAPTER 8

ENGLAND HERO

After playing for the England youth teams, Harry made his senior England debut on **19 March 2015** in a **EURO 2016** qualifier against **Lithuania.**

Harry came on as sub and within **two minutes** he headed in a cross from **Raheem Sterling.**

BOFF!

WORLD CUP 2018

Harry was made **England captain** for the **2018 World Cup** in **Russia**.

IT WAS AN INCREDIBLE HONOUR!

18 JUNE 2018

Tunisia 1-2 England

*Harry scored **both** goals as England beat Tunisia in their opening game of the tournament.*

24 JUNE 2018

England 6-1 Panama

*Harry scored a **hat-trick** as Panama were thrashed in England's biggest ever World Cup win.*

Harry is the youngest player to captain England at a World Cup.

On **3 July 2018**, England faced **Colombia** in the round of 16. Harry scored a **penalty**, but Colombia equalised to make it **1-1**. The game went to a penalty shoot-out.

England **had never won** a World Cup penalty shoot-out . . . except this time,

THEY DID!

England reached a **World Cup semi-final** for the first time in **28 years.** In the end, they lost to **Croatia,** but Harry and the young team had done **brilliantly.**

HARRY'S SIX GOALS WON HIM THE WORLD CUP GOLDEN BOOT:

Harry is the first English player to win the award since Gary Lineker in *1990.*

Another one!

Harry joins some famous names in scoring for **England** at the **World Cup.**

SCORED WORLD CUP HAT-TRICKS

HARRY KANE
2018
6 goals

GARY LINEKER
1986 and 1990
10 goals

ENGLAND WILL WIN THE CUP
by
I. M. Sure

SIR GEOFF HURST
1966 and 1970
5 goals

WORLD CUP WINNERS, 1966

SIR BOBBY CHARLTON
1962 and 1966
4 goals

LAST MINUTE GOALS by Justin Time

RECORD BREAKER?

Harry had scored 26 international goals by the age of 26.

HARRY KANE
2015-

45 caps — 32 goals

MICHAEL OWEN
1998-2008

89 caps — 40 goals

WAYNE ROONEY
2003-2018

120 caps — 53 goals

COULD HARRY BECOME ENGLAND'S RECORD GOALSCORER?

ALAN SHEARER *1992-2000* — 63 caps, 30 goals

GARY LINEKER *1984-1992* — 80 caps, 48 goals

JIMMY GREAVES *1959-1967* — 57 caps, 44 goals

BOBBY CHARLTON *1958-1970* — 106 caps, 49 goals

HARRY KANE MBE

In **2019,** Harry was awarded an **MBE** (Member of Order of the British Empire) for his **services to world football.** In other words, scoring goals for England!

Prince William presented him with the medal.

PRINCE WILLIAM –
ASTON VILLA FAN

CHAPTER 9

PREMIER KING

PREMIER LEAGUE 2017-18

Harry didn't score in the first **three** games of the season, but then he scored **TWICE** in each of these matches:

9 SEPTEMBER
Everton 0-3 Tottenham

23 SEPTEMBER
West Ham 2-3 Tottenham

CHRISTMAS GOALS

Harry scored all **THREE goals** against Burnley just before **Christmas 2017.** Then, incredibly, he scored another **hat-trick** on **Boxing Day** as Spurs beat Southampton **5-2.**

RECORD BREAKER

Between **January** and **December** 2017, **Harry** scored . . .

. . . **39** Premier League goals (breaking Alan Shearer's record of 35)

. . . **six hat-tricks** (the most in one year)

. . . a total of **56 goals** for club and country.

100 GOALS

Harry scored his **100th Premier League** goal against Liverpool on 4 February 2018.

DELE ALLI

IT WAS HIS **141ST** APPEARANCE.

Only Alan Shearer has scored 100 goals in a shorter amount of time!

MY FIRST FOOTBALL FACTS

BALL

CHAPTER 10

EUROPEAN NIGHTS

EUROPA LEAGUE HIGHLIGHTS

15 DECEMBER 2011

GROUP STAGE

**Shamrock Rovers 0
Tottenham 4**

*Harry scored his **first ever** Spurs goal in the 91st minute of this match against the Irish champions.*

23 OCTOBER 2014

GROUP STAGE
TOTTENHAM 5-1 ASTERAS TRIPOLIS

*Harry scored a right-footed shot, a tap-in and a header for his **first** European **hat-trick**.*

Harry has a total of **10 goals** in eight Europa League matches.

GREATEST GOAL #2

13 SEPTEMBER 2017
CHAMPIONS LEAGUE GROUP STAGE
Tottenham 3-1 Borussia Dortmund

This was a **big game** in a tough group.

Harry got the ball at the halfway line, lost one

player, got past another and . . .

BOOM

. . . he scored with his **LEFT foot**

from an angle.

Harry scored against Dortmund again in a last-16 match in the **2018-19** season. It was his **24th European goal** and made him Tottenham's **highest ever scorer** in Europe.

WHACK!

Harry was injured for much of the **2018-19** season, but his **five Champions League** goals helped Spurs reach the **final** for the **first time** in their history.

EUROPEAN GOAL RECORD

SEASON	COMPETITION	APPEARANCES	GOALS
2011–12	EUROPA LEAGUE	1	1
2014–15	EUROPA LEAGUE	5	7
2015–16	EUROPA LEAGUE	2	2
2016–17	CHAMPIONS LEAGUE	2	2
2017–18	CHAMPIONS LEAGUE	4	7
2018–19	CHAMPIONS LEAGUE	4	5

CHAPTER 11

ONE OF OUR OWN

TOP SPUR

	APPEARANCES	GOALS
HARRY KANE	278	181
JERMAIN DEFOE	363	143
TEDDY SHERINGHAM	277	124

HARRY KANE
2011-

JERMAIN DEFOE
2004-2008
2009-2014

TEDDY SHERINGHAM
1992-1997
2001-2003

104

HOW DOES HARRY COMPARE WITH SOME FAMOUS TOTTENHAM PLAYERS FROM THE PAST?

138 | 80 | 490 | 110 | 379 | 266

GARY LINEKER
1989-1992

GLENN HODDLE
1975-1987

JIMMY GREAVES
1961-1970

SQUAD GOALS!

HARRY KANE
FORWARD

278 appearances

181 goals

30 assists

SON HEUNG-MIN
FORWARD

213 appearances

77 goals

45 assists

CHRISTIAN ERIKSEN
MIDFIELDER

302 appearances

69 goals

89 assists

DELE ALLI
MIDFIELDER

206 appearances

60 goals

52 assists

DID SOMEONE SAY **SQUID** GOALS?

STEVEN SQUID - striker for Cephalopod F.C.

107

"HARRY'S A TOP QUALITY PLAYER AND HE'S GOING TO BE AROUND FOR A LONG TIME."

Alan Shearer

108

CHAPTER 12

THE HURRICANE

PREMIER LEAGUE GOALS

SEASON	APPEARANCES	GOALS
2012-13	1	0
2013-14	10	3
2014-15	34	21
2015-16	38	25
2016-17	30	29
2017-18	37	30
2018-19	28	17
2019-20	20	11
TOTAL	198	136

ALL COMPETITION GOALS

SEASON	APPEARANCES	GOALS
2011-12	6	1
2012-13	1	0
2013-14	19	4
2014-15	51	31
2015-16	50	28
2016-17	38	35
2017-18	48	41
2018-19	40	24
2019-20	25	17
TOTAL	278	181

ENGLAND GOALS

YEAR	APPEARANCES	GOALS
2015	8	3
2016	9	2
2017	6	7
2018	12	8
2019	10	12
TOTAL	45	32

In **2019**, Harry **scored more goals** in one calendar year than any **England player** for **90 years**.

THUMP!

Harry scored in **every single match** of the **EURO 2020** qualifiers. No other England player has done that in **any** qualifying campaign.

HONOURS AND AWARDS

LEAGUE CUP RUNNER-UP
2014-15

CHAMPIONS LEAGUE RUNNER-UP
2018-19

PREMIER LEAGUE PLAYER OF THE MONTH
JANUARY 2015
FEBRUARY 2015
MARCH 2016
FEBRUARY 2017
SEPTEMBER 2017
DECEMBER 2017

PFA TEAM OF THE YEAR
2014-15
2015-16
2016-17
2017-18

HARRY VERSUS . . .

Harry's goal against **Cardiff City** in January 2019 made him the first player to score against **every Premier League** team he's played.

WOW!

That was until he played against *Sheffield United!*

HARRY'S FAVOURITE PREMIER LEAGUE TEAMS TO SCORE AGAINST:

TEAM	GAMES	GOALS
LEICESTER CITY	9	14
ARSENAL	11	10
SOUTHAMPTON	12	9
EVERTON	9	9
STOKE CITY	9	9
WEST HAM	11	8
BURNLEY	9	8
WEST BROM	7	7
BOURNEMOUTH	7	7
LIVERPOOL	11	6

Tottenham were playing the Italian giants **Juventus** in a pre-season friendly in Singapore. It was **2–2** in stoppage time, when **Harry struck the ball** from the halfway line.

BOOM!

THE BALL SAILED INTO THE BACK OF THE NET!

DID YOU KNOW?

Harry's two dogs, **Brady** and **Wilson** are named after American footballers **Tom Brady** and **Russell Wilson.**

BRADY

WILSON

He loves playing **golf,** usually with his **brother Charlie.**

He threw the first pitch at a **Chicago Cubs** baseball game in **2014.**

Harry says **Ryan Gosling** should play him in a film of his life!

WORLD'S MOST *VALUABLE* PLAYERS

PLAYER	CLUB	ESTIMATED VALUE
KYLIAN MBAPPÉ	PARIS ST GERMAIN	*£180 million*
NEYMAR	PARIS ST GERMAIN	*£162 million*
MOHAMED SALAH	LIVERPOOL	*£135 million*
HARRY KANE	TOTTENHAM HOTSPUR	*£135 million*

PLAYER	CLUB	ESTIMATED VALUE
EDEN HAZARD	REAL MADRID	*£135 million*
LIONEL MESSI	BARCELONA	*£135 million*
RAHEEM STERLING	MANCHESTER CITY	*£126 million*
ANTOINE GRIEZMANN	BARCELONA	*£117 million*
KEVIN DE BRUYNE	MANCHESTER CITY	*£117 million*
SADIO MANÉ	LIVERPOOL	*£108 million*

QUIZ TIME!

How much do you know about **Harry Kane?** Try this quiz to find out, then test your friends!

1. What is the name of the local team that Harry played for?

---

2. How many goals did Harry score in all competitions in 2014-15?

---

3. Which famous England captain went to the same school as Harry?

---

4. How many Premier League Golden Boots has Harry won?

---

5. Which American footballer is Harry's hero?

----

6. How many goals did Harry score against Leicester City in one game in May 2017?

----

7. Harry won the Golden Boot at the 2018 World Cup. How many goals did he score?

----

8. Harry scored a record number of goals in the calendar year of 2017. How many was it?

----

9. How many clubs did Harry go out on loan to?

----

10. How many goals did Harry score for England in 2019?

The answers are on the next page *but no peeking!*

ANSWERS

1. Ridgeway Rovers
2. 31
3. David Beckham
4. Two
5. Tom Brady
6. Four
7. Six
8. 56
9. Four
10. 12

HARRY KANE:
WORDS YOU NEED TO KNOW

Premier League
The top football league in England.

Golden Boot
Award presented to the top scorer in a competition.

PFA
Professional Footballers' Association

UEFA Champions League
European club competition held every year. The winner is the best team in Europe.

UEFA Europa League
The second-tier European club competition.

ABOUT THE AUTHORS

Simon's first job was at the Science Museum, making paper aeroplanes and blowing bubbles big enough for your dad to stand in. Since then he's written all sorts of books about the stuff he likes, from dinosaurs and rockets, to llamas, loud music and of course, football. Simon has supported Ipswich Town since they won the FA Cup in 1978 (it's true - look it up) and once sat next to Rio Ferdinand on a train. He lives in Kent with his wife and daughter, two tortoises and a cat.

Dan has drawn silly pictures since he could hold a crayon. Then he grew up and started making books about stuff like trucks, space, people's jobs, *Doctor Who* and *Star Wars*. Dan remembers Ipswich Town winning the FA cup but he didn't watch it because he was too busy making a Viking ship out of brown paper. As a result, he knows more about Vikings than football. Dan lives in Suffolk with his wife, son, daughter and a dog that takes him for very long walks.